UNPREDICTABLE! FROM HEN TO EAGLE

FROM THE SHELLS OF FEAR TO THE HEIGHTS OF YOUR PURPOSE

MARÍA ISABEL RODRÍGUEZ

📖 INDEX

📖 Prologue	1
1. 📖 The Shell of Fear	5
2. 📖 From Chicken to Eagle: The Change of Mindset	9
3. 📖 The Wings of the Process	15
4. 📖 Breaking Out of the Shell	20
5. 📖 The Flight of the Eagle	25
6. 📖 Being Unstoppable	29
7. 📖 The Eagle's Nest: Place of Training	35
8. 📖 The Eagle's Renewal: Dying to Fly Again	40
9. 📖 Eagles that inspire others	44
10. 📖 Stay Steady in Your Unpredictable Flight	49
11. 📖 Eagles in the Bible: Lessons from the Word	52
12. 📖 Unpredictable Leadership: Leading from Above	57
13. 📖 Leading with Eagle Wings	60
14. 📖 The Price of Flying High: What No One Tells You About the Eagle's Path	66
15. 📖 Achieve It! Steps to Maintain the Eagle's Flight	69
16. 📖 When Heaven Opens Your Wings	74
17. 📖 Unpredictable: The flight that changes your story	78
18. 📖 Final Chapter – Your flight begins today	81
📖 Additional Resources	87
✦ Spaces for your reflections	89
📖 About the author	95

Title: Unpredictable *From Hen to Eagle*

Author: María Isabel Rodríguez

First edition: 2025

ISBN: 979-8-9934560-4-1

✦ Copyright

© 2025 María Isabel Rodríguez.

All rights reserved. No part of this publication may be reproduced, stored in a retrieval system, or transmitted in any form or by any means, electronic, mechanical, photocopying, recording, or otherwise, without the prior written permission of the author, except for brief quotations used in critical reviews or articles.

✦ Acknowledgments

To God, for being my strength, my inspiration, and the wind that sustains my wings.

To my family, for walking with me through every process and believing in the vision.

To my church, for being my place of formation and perseverance.

To all those who, with their words of encouragement or even their criticisms, contributed to making this book possible.

✦ Editing and design

- Writing and development: **María Isabel Rodríguez**
- Editorial edition: *Independent*

✦ **Important note**

This book is based on personal experiences, spiritual reflections, and biblical foundations. Its purpose is to inspire and edify, not to replace professional counseling or personalized pastoral care.

To You, my beloved God, who rescued me when I still didn't know how to fly. Thank You for showing me in my struggles and falls that You were always there, holding my wings. To You be all the glory, for without Your grace this book would not exist. You are the true author of every page, the source of my strength, and the air that propels me to fly.

To my beloved husband and my children, who walked and flew with me even through storms. You were my support in difficult times and my joy in victorious ones. Each of you is part of my journey; with your smiles, your prayers, and your love, you reminded me that I was never alone.

To my extended family and to all those who taught me, even with their criticism or rejection, that processes are necessary. Today I can say that even the pain was part of God's plan to shape me and give me new wings.

My church, my nest, and my training ground. There I learned to serve, to obey, and to persevere. Thank you for being the place where God shaped my character and where I learned that true faithfulness isn't measured in easy times, but in moments of trial. Persevering through difficulties made me understand that it is possible, that God always keeps His word.

And finally, I dedicate this book to you, reader, who may feel trapped in a shell of fear, pain, or insecurity today. This book is to remind you that there is an eagle inside you. Even if others have made you feel like a chicken, God designed you to fly. I pray that each page will be a boost of faith, a breath of hope, and a reminder that your story has only just begun.

📖 PROLOGUE

When I first started walking with God, I was inexperienced in everything related to Him. I had no knowledge; I felt like a lost chicken in a world full of disappointments, infidelity, and struggles. But God already had plans that I couldn't yet see.

In my book *Today I am stronger than yesterday* I share my struggles, failures, disappointments, falls, infidelity, and above all, my encounter with God. That was my beginning. I realized that the wounds weren't meant to destroy me, but to push me to discover who I was in Christ.

When I began my discipleship journey, I worked in ministries and departments with great fear and difficulty. Many didn't see that God had a plan for me. At times, I had to endure shouting, stop myself, and didn't dare to defend myself. I felt like a weak chicken in a coop full of criticism. But my pastor saw an eagle in me and decided to disciple me, open doors for me, and show me that there was indeed a greater purpose.

Over the years I understood that my struggles were just my shell. And that shell was designed to break.

That understanding led me to discover something powerful: life with God is **unpredictable.** He surprises us, lifts us up when we think all is lost, and teaches us to fly in places we never imagined. Being "unpredictable" is not instability; it is being a living testament that God uses the unexpected to take us higher.

We often think that the safest place to grow is the church. However, the reality is that we have also been hurt there, received hurtful words, and faced wounding attitudes. Many, for fear of being hurt again, choose to hide in a shell of fear and insecurity. That shell becomes a prison that prevents them from seeing beyond the pain.

In my own experience, I understood that those wounds don't define who I am, but rather reveal how much I need to discover the strength God has already placed within me. The more I took refuge in fear, the more I felt like a chicken: limited, unable to take flight, always looking at the ground. But when I discovered that this shell wasn't my destiny, but only a stage of development, something began to transform inside me.

This book, *Unpredictable: From Hen to Eagle* It was born to show you that there is an eagle inside you. Even if you feel you can't fly now, within your heart are wings ready to rise above the storms. A hen runs from the rain, but an eagle faces it and uses the storm to soar even higher.

In the pages that follow, you'll find stories of highs and lows, moments of pain and glory. But above all, you'll find practical and spiritual tools to help you break free from fear and begin to soar with vision, purpose, and freedom.

My wish is that as you read this book, you will feel God's call to break out of your shell, leave insecurity behind, and discover that you were created to be unpredictable, **unstoppable and unforgettable.**

Welcome to this transformative journey. It's time to stop walking like a chicken and start flying like an eagle.

CHAPTER 1
📖 THE SHELL OF FEAR

Fear is like a shell that encloses and limits us. Many of us have suffered wounds in the church or in life that leave deep scars. Harsh words, rejection, criticism, or indifference fill us with insecurity and make us believe we have no worth.

I myself worked in ministries and departments with a lot of fear. I endured shouting, awkward silences, and moments when I didn't even dare to speak up to defend myself. That was my shell: a place where I hid from my insecurities, but also a space where God was shaping my character.

An eggshell is not a destination, it's a stage. The chick wasn't born to stay inside, but to break out. So too are we: what imprisons us today is merely a process to push us to be reborn into our purpose.

MARÍA ISABEL RODRÍGUEZ

We are all born with a purpose, but often the first thing we face in life is not confidence, but fear. Fear is like a shell: hard on the outside, but fragile on the inside. It encloses us, limits us, and prevents us from seeing what truly lies beyond.

This book, *Unpredictable: From Hen to Eagle* It is an invitation to discover that what seems like your limit is, in reality, the harbinger of your spiritual rebirth. The fear you face today is not your end: it is the sign that you are about to spread your wings.

THE WOUNDS THAT MARK US

Some of the most painful blows don't come from the world, but from people we claim to love and who claim to love God. Words of rejection, indifference, or even unfair judgments wound us deeply. These experiences create insecurity and make us think, "If this happened to me here, what will happen to me out there?"

The enemy knows that if he can fill us with fear, we will never discover the power and calling that God has placed within us. So we begin to hide, to live half-lives, like chickens that prefer to stay on the ground instead of trying to fly.

THE HIDDEN POWER IN THE SHELL

A hen is content to stay on the ground, but an eagle is born to conquer the heights. The fear you feel today is not your end; it's a sign that something greater inside you is about to break.

God allows us to go through wounds and trials not to destroy us, but to shape us. Just as a chick struggles against its own shell to break free and be born, you need to face your fear to emerge into the light of your purpose.

REAL LIFE EXAMPLES

- A young woman who was hurt by leaders in her church decided never to return. But in the midst of her loneliness, she discovered that God had never left her, and little by little she began to heal and serve again. Today she is a woman who guides others to find restoration.
- A man who always felt insecure when speaking in public admitted that he "wasn't cut out for it." However, God lifted him up, and now he preaches with power. What seemed like a limitation became his greatest strength.

These testimonies remind us that fear is not an end point, it is the beginning of a process.

MARÍA ISABEL RODRÍGUEZ

REFLECTION

In what area of your life do you feel trapped in a shell? What wounds or fears are holding you back? Acknowledge them, bring them before God, and begin to see them as part of your growth process.

📌 Practical exercise for the reader:

Write down on a piece of paper the fears that have limited you the most. Then, pray and declare aloud:

> *"This shell is not my destiny. I am being trained to fly like an eagle."*

CHAPTER 2
📖 FROM CHICKEN TO EAGLE: THE CHANGE OF MINDSET

✦ **T**hought for your life

Changing your mindset means understanding that you weren't designed to live a limited life, always looking down like a chicken in a coop. Your true identity lies above, where eagles soar with vision and purpose.

This is the central message of *Unpredictable: From Hen to Eagle* Your life can surprise you and others when you decide to break free from routine, fear, and insecurity. God's unpredictability lies in taking what is weak and making it strong, what is rejected and giving it purpose, and what is hidden and raising it to new heights.

Today your unpredictable flight begins: don't return to the corral, because your wings were created for the sky.

The difference between a chicken and an eagle is not in the wings, but in the mentality.

- The hen always looks at the ground, lives in safety, and limits herself to the immediate.
- The eagle fixes its eyes on high, it does not fear the storm and always seeks heights.

RENEWING OUR MINDS WITH THE WORD

The Bible says:

> *"But those who wait on the Lord will renew their strength; they will soar on wings like eagles; they will run and not grow weary, they will walk and not be faint."*
>
> (Isaiah 40:31)

This verse speaks not only of strength, but also of a change of mindset. Waiting on God is not passivity; it is trusting, letting go of fear, and believing that our identity is in Him.

By renewing your mind, you will stop thinking, "I can't, I'm no good, I'm not enough," and you will begin to declare, "In Christ I am more than a conqueror, I was created to soar high, my past does not define my future."

My pastor saw an eagle in me when I only saw myself as a chicken. He decided to disciple me, open doors for me, and teach me to see what God saw. Little by little, I began to replace my thoughts of defeat with truths from the Word. Although at times I felt like I was saying yes to everything, that process taught me obedience and discipline.

KEYS TO CHANGING YOUR MINDSET:

1. Identify your chicken thoughts.
2. Replace them with eagle thoughts.
3. Surround yourself with people who inspire you to grow.
4. Dare to take steps even if you are afraid.

📌 PRACTICAL EXERCISE: MAKE TWO COLUMNS IN YOUR NOTEBOOK:

- Chicken thoughts.
- Eagle thoughts.

Each day, replace one of the first thoughts with an eagle thought based on the Bible.

One of the greatest battles we fight is not against what others tell us, but against what we ourselves believe about ourselves. Fear, insecurity, and hurt can trap us in a chicken mentality, even though God has already designed us to be eagles.

MARÍA ISABEL RODRÍGUEZ

THE CHICKEN MENTALITY

The hen represents a limited life:

- Always look down, searching for food on the earth.
- It doesn't risk flying, it barely makes small hops.
- He settles for what is immediate and safe.
- She lives surrounded by noise, but without vision.

This is how many Christians live: trapped by "what others will say," by spiritual routine, by the comfort of the familiar. Not because they lack wings, but because they have never tried to spread them.

THE EAGLE'S VISION

The eagle, on the other hand, has a different mentality:

- She raises her eyes and fixes her gaze upwards.
- He does not fear the storm; he uses it to fly higher.
- He has a broad vision; he doesn't get distracted by superficial things.
- It rises on its own, if necessary, but always firmly.

The difference between a chicken and an eagle is not in the wings, but in the mentality.

PRACTICAL STEPS TO CHANGE YOUR MINDSET

1. Identify your chicken thoughts
2. Make a list of internal phrases like: "I am not capable", "I will never change", "I always fail".
3. Counter them with eagle thoughts
4. Replace each lie with a biblical truth: "I can do all things through Christ," "I am a new creation," "The Lord is my strength."
5. Surround yourself with vision
6. Your environment influences your mindset. Seek out mentors, leaders, and friends who inspire you to grow.
7. Dare to try it
8. The eagle learns to fly by taking the leap. Don't wait to feel ready, take the first step and trust that God will hold your wings.

INSPIRING TESTIMONY

I remember the case of a woman who saw herself as "not very spiritual" because she didn't sing, preach, or have any visible talents. She always considered herself less than others in the church. One day she realized that her talent was listening and giving advice, and God raised her up as a counselor for hurting women. When she changed her mindset, she discovered she had wings bigger than she ever imagined.

REFLECTION

Your identity isn't defined by what others have said about you, but by what God says about you. Every time you think like a chicken, ask yourself: Is this what God thinks of me, or is it what my fear makes me believe?

CHAPTER 3

📖 THE WINGS OF THE PROCESS

Pain and trials forge our wings. No one is born flying: we all need to be trained.

Like the eagle that plucks out its old feathers and strikes its beak to renew itself, we too go through processes that hurt us, but that prepare us to fly higher.

In my book *Giving up is not an option* I recount how many times I wanted to give up. However, I learned that pain wasn't a sign of defeat, but rather a training ground for my faith. Every tear strengthened me, every wound taught me something, every fall pushed me to depend more on God.

When we see an eagle soaring high, majestic and free, we forget that before getting there it has to go through a process. No one is born flying; we all need to learn to spread our wings.

In the Christian life, that learning takes place amidst trials, wounds, and struggles.

The message of *Unpredictable: From Hen to Eagle* This is precisely it: what seems like your end is just a transition. The unpredictable thing about God is that He uses what hurts to renew you, what weighs you down to strengthen your wings, and what wounds you to prepare you to fly higher.

Every process is part of your training. Don't be afraid: what you cry for today will be the strength that makes you fly tomorrow.

LESSONS FROM THE PROCESS:

- You are not defined by your falls.
- The brokenness opens space for healing.
- Loneliness can be a school of intimacy with God.

THE TRIALS THAT SHAPE US

Many desire the strength of the eagle, but they don't want the process that develops it. Difficulties are not a punishment; they are the training ground for our faith.

- Every tear strengthens our dependence on God.
- Every wound teaches us to heal and then to heal others.

- Every fall shows us that we cannot fly alone.

What seems like a loss is, in reality, a stage of development.

PAIN AS A TEACHER

The eagle, in order to grow, goes through moments of pain:

- When its old feathers are no longer useful, it must pluck them out to make room for new ones.
- When its claws wear down, it must strike the rock until they are renewed.
- When its beak weakens, it breaks it against the mountain so that a new one can grow.

That process is painful, but necessary to prolong life and regain strength. Likewise, God allows us to go through seasons where we feel like everything is falling apart, but in reality, He is renewing us.

LESSONS AMIDST THE LOWS

1. You are not defined by a fall: an interrupted flight does not mean you were not born to fly.

2. Brokenness opens space for healing: when you acknowledge your wound, God can restore it.
3. Loneliness can be a school: sometimes God sets the eagle apart to teach it to depend only on Him.

TECHNIQUES FOR GROWING IN THE MIDST OF THE PROCESS

- Forgive: forgiveness breaks the chains that bind you to the past.
- Pray sincerely: not with pretty words, but with your truth before God.
- Surround yourself with support: find a healthy community that empowers you, not holds you back.
- Wait on God: patience is the air that strengthens your wings.

REAL-LIFE EXAMPLE

A ministry leader was unfairly humiliated and criticized. He considered giving up and abandoning his calling. However, in that process, he discovered the depth of his relationship with God. Today, he preaches with an authority he didn't have before the hurt. The pain didn't destroy him; it renewed him.

REFLECTION

Every process is like a strong wind: it can knock you to the ground or it can lift you to the heights. The difference lies in whether you choose to give up like a chicken or spread your wings like an eagle.

📌 PRACTICAL EXERCISE FOR THE READER:

Think back to a wound or ordeal that marked your life. Write it in your notebook and answer:

- What did I learn from this experience?
- How did it make me stronger?
- What part of my life was renewed in that process?

Declare aloud:

> *"My wounds don't stop me, my wings are being formed."*

CHAPTER 4
📖 BREAKING OUT OF THE SHELL

Breaking out of the shell is uncomfortable and painful, but it's the only way to grow.

Over the years, I began to trust myself more, and my family progressed with me. They, too, decided to walk and fly. That was a pivotal moment: I not only broke out of my shell, but I inspired my family to do the same.

The shell represents fear, insecurity, and the limitations that keep us trapped. Inside it, we feel protected, but also stagnant. The shell is comfortable because it prevents us from facing risks, but it also robs us of the opportunity to grow.

The unpredictability of this process—and here lies the heart of *Unpredictable: From Hen to Eagle* — the thing is, we never know when or how that shell will break. Sometimes we think it will happen in a moment of strength, but God allows it in the midst of our weaknesses. Other times we believe we are about to give up, and that is when the true birth occurs.

How to break out of the shell:

- Face your fears one by one: write down what your biggest fear is and decide to take a step against it.
- Accept that pain is part of birth: chicks don't hatch without effort. Your new season requires pushing forward.
- Seek spiritual support: surround yourself with people who encourage you instead of reinforcing your insecurities.
- Declare your new identity: you are not a slave to fear, you are a child of God, called to fly high.

Breaking out of your shell is not the end of your story, it's the beginning of an unpredictable flight.

THE DANGER OF STAYING INSIDE

A chick that never hatches dies. Likewise, a Christian who never faces their fears misses out on experiencing the fullness of their calling.

- The shell can be a failure mindset.

- It may be the voice of the past repeating: "You can't, you're no good."
- It could be the fear of the unknown.

Staying in it may feel safe, but in reality it is deadly for our purpose.

THE MOMENT OF THE BREAKUP

Breaking out of your shell isn't easy. It requires strength, persistence, and determination. It's an internal process that begins with a conviction: "I no longer belong here."

- It's not just about stepping out of your comfort zone, but about accepting the discomfort of growth.
- It's not about ignoring the pain, but about going through it trusting that something new awaits me.

Jesus said:

> "Unless a grain of wheat falls into the earth and dies, it remains alone; but if it dies, it bears much fruit."
> (Juan 12:24)

That dying is breaking the shell to bear fruit.

REAL-LIFE EXAMPLE

A man lived for years trapped in the shell of addiction. He felt he could never escape, that he would always be the same. But one day he decided to take a step: to seek help and confess his struggle. That act was like the first blow to his shell. Today he lives free and helps others break free from theirs.

REFLECTION

The shell that imprisons you today will be tomorrow's testament to your freedom. Do not fear the pain of breaking it, for it is the price of your birth into a new life.

Every challenge you face is different, but they all serve the same purpose: to prepare you for flight. Perhaps today you feel trapped, limited, or invisible, but that place is not your destiny. God has given you eagle wings, and although it may seem unpredictable, the exact moment will come when you will break free from what limits you and take flight.

   Remember: the shell doesn't define you, it only announces that you are about to be born into a new season.

📌 PRACTICAL EXERCISE FOR THE READER:

Make a list of the "shells" in your life (fears, insecurities, habits). Choose one and decide to take a concrete step this week to break it. Pray like this:

> *"Lord, give me the strength of an eagle to break free from every shell that limits me. Today I choose to be reborn into my true identity."*

CHAPTER 5
📖 THE FLIGHT OF THE EAGLE

The eagle does not flee from the storm; it faces it and uses it to soar. What is destruction to others, is promotion to it.

That's how I also discovered that the storms in my life were platforms. When our pastor proposed we start a ministry in an unfamiliar place, we were afraid. It was new territory, starting from scratch. But there we learned that the difference is clear: the hen runs away, the eagle says yes even though it trembles.

Breaking out of the shell is just the beginning. Once you discover your wings, it's time to learn how to use them. The eagle doesn't settle for small leaps; she soars, and she does so in a unique way: she uses what others fear to reach new heights.

STORMS AS AN OPPORTUNITY

The eagle spreads its wings and lets the strong winds propel it upwards. Likewise, life's problems and trials are not signs of defeat, but platforms for growth.

- The financial crisis can teach you about management.
- Rejection can teach you to depend on God's acceptance.
- Loneliness can lead you to a deeper intimacy with the Holy Spirit.

The secret lies in perspective: do you see the storm as your end or as your rise?

And this is where the message of Unpredictable: From Hen to EagleIt comes alive: no one expects your greatest strength to emerge in the midst of a storm, but it is precisely there that you discover your wings are ready. God's unpredictability lies in transforming your worst winds into the very ones that lift you highest.

LESSONS FROM FLYING

1. Spread your wings: the eagle doesn't fight against the wind, it embraces it. You don't need to fight against

everything either; learn to surrender to God and let His strength propel you.
2. Soar higher than your problems: the higher the eagle flies, the less the storm can reach it. You weren't called to live at the level of your problems, but above them.
3. Maintain your vision: an eagle can see for miles. Don't lose your focus amidst the turbulence.

BIBLICAL EXAMPLE

Joseph was sold by his brothers, unjustly accused, and imprisoned. Everything seemed like a storm that was sinking him, but in reality, every wind was lifting him toward his destiny in the palace of Egypt. What appeared to be his destruction was the very force that propelled him to fulfill his purpose.

REAL-LIFE EXAMPLE

A woman faced an unexpected illness. Instead of giving up, she began writing about her journey and sharing her faith. Today, her story inspires thousands. The storm that could have destroyed her propelled her to new heights.

REFLECTION

Storms are inevitable, but your response determines whether they destroy you or lift you up. The chicken runs away and hides; the eagle spreads its wings and soars higher. You decide which mindset you'll have.

Every storm you face has a hidden purpose. Do not fear when the winds blow strong, for they are not signs of your downfall, but God's invitation to rise.

The unpredictable thing about the storm is that it doesn't come to destroy you, but to remind you that you were designed to fly higher.

📌 **Practical exercise for the reader:**

Think about the strongest storm you are experiencing today. Write it in your notebook and answer:

- What is this storm teaching me?
- How can it be an impetus for growth in my faith and purpose?

Declare aloud:

"I don't fear the storm, it inspires me to fly higher."

CHAPTER 6
📖 BEING UNSTOPPABLE

Becoming an eagle doesn't mean there will be no more trials, but rather that you now know how to face them. What once held you back no longer has power over you. When you discover your true identity in God, you understand that nothing and no one can stop what He has placed within you.

The apostle Paul declared it with conviction:

Romans 8:37 reminds us:

> *"No, in all these things we are more than conquerors through him who loved us."*

That is the identity of an eagle: victorious, renewed, and with vision.

Today I can proclaim with certainty: *"I am stronger than yesterday."* What were once failures are now scars that tell of victory. Each wound became a reminder that I survived, that I was renewed, and that now I fly higher.

In my first book, I shared my struggles, falls, failures, disappointments, even infidelity, and above all, my encounter with God. At that time, I still felt like a chicken held back by fear. But in this work, I confirmed something greater: all those experiences didn't stop me; they were the fuel that strengthened my wings.

The unpredictability of God—and what gives this book its name, *Unpredictable: From Hen to Eagle*— He takes what seemed like your end and turns it into the beginning of your greatest flight. No one expected purpose to emerge from my ruins; no one imagined strength would be born from my tears. But God, in His power, transformed every fall into momentum, every pain into preparation, and every fear into faith.

Today I do not speak from defeat, but from testimony: what began as a chicken is now an eagle that does not stop.

You are unpredictable because what seemed like the end of your story is just the beginning of the flight that God designed for you.

THE IDENTITY OF THE EAGLE IN CHRIST

Fear makes you believe you were weak, but in Christ you understand that you are strong.

Insecurity makes you think you were insignificant, but God reminds you that you are his beloved child.

The wounds made you feel broken, but now they are scars that tell a story of victory.

📖 FROM WOUND TO TESTIMONY

Your past struggles are not a source of shame; they fuel your purpose. Every wound becomes a message, every fall a lesson, every tear a ministry. What once made you hide is now what drives you to inspire others.

An eagle doesn't hide its scars; it uses them as evidence of survival and triumph. Its wings not only reflect majesty but also show that it has weathered storms, winds, and battles. So too are we: our marks are not signs of defeat, but banners of victory.

The unpredictability of God—and the essence of *Unpredictable: From Hen to Eagle*— It transforms what seemed to be your greatest wound into your greatest testimony. No one expected that what broke you would become your platform. No one imagined that the tears you shed would be a source of hope for others. But God uses the unlikely, the fragile, and the rejected to display His glory.

Your wounds are proof that you are unpredictable: what was meant to destroy you now proclaims that you are unstoppable.

Today you can raise your head and declare:

- My scars don't embarrass me, they identify me as a survivor.
- My defeats don't define me, they taught me to fly.
- My tears didn't sink me, they were the water that nourished my purpose.

Once you were a hen, limited by insecurity. Today you are an eagle, unpredictable in God's hands, soaring over the same storms others feared.

KEYS TO LIVING AN UNSTOPPABLE LIFE

1. Keep your sights set high: don't go back to living like a chicken, with your eyes on the ground. Your focus should be on the sky.
2. Embrace your process: remember that the storms and the pain were just training your wings.
3. Share your flight: an unstoppable eagle doesn't fly just for itself, but to guide others to fly.

4. Declare your identity daily: do not let the enemy sow doubts; proclaim who you are in Christ.

"Today I can say that I am stronger than yesterday".

BIBLICAL EXAMPLE

Peter denied Jesus three times out of fear. He was a "chicken" hiding in insecurity. But after being restored by Christ and filled with the Holy Spirit, he rose up like an "eagle," preaching boldly. Thousands were saved by his message. What once held him back no longer had power over him.

REAL-LIFE EXAMPLE

A young man who grew up hearing he'd never amount to anything ended up believing it. But an encounter with God transformed his identity. Today he's an entrepreneur, a leader, and a mentor to other young people who, like him, once thought they were chickens. His life demonstrates that when you embrace your identity in Christ, you are unstoppable.

FINAL REFLECTION

An eagle doesn't ask permission to fly; it simply opens its wings and takes off. You don't need everyone's approval; you need God's confirmation. When you choose to live like an eagle, no storm, wound, or fear can stop you.

📌 PRACTICAL EXERCISE FOR THE READER:

Make a list of the things that used to hold you back (fear, insecurity, hurts, voices from the past). Now write next to each one how God has transformed it into strength.

Declare aloud:

> *"I am unstoppable because Christ lives in me. My wounds do not hold me back, my past does not limit me, and my purpose has no boundaries."*

CHAPTER 7

📖 THE EAGLE'S NEST: PLACE OF TRAINING

The nest is the place of formation. My church was that nest. There I learned to serve, to obey, and to remain.

I never ran away, even though there was pain. I didn't jump from church to church. I stayed in the place God assigned me. That's where I was formed.

Over the years I understood that my mission was not only to grow, but to help others grow. Today I dedicate my life to discipleship and developing eagles.

When an eagle hatches, the first thing it encounters is not the open sky, but the nest. This nest is where it learns to grow, to feed, and to develop its wings. However, it is not its final destination, but rather a place of formation.

Likewise, when we emerge from our shell of fear and insecurity, God places us in a nest: our church, our discipleship, our spiritual journey. The nest isn't always comfortable, but it's necessary..

✦ THE VALUE OF STAYING

Many birds abandon their nest when they feel uncomfortable. But the eagle doesn't send its young out into flight until they are strong. Leaving prematurely is risking their lives.

The nest is discipline.

The nest is correction.

The nest is a formation.

Staying amidst trials and corrections wasn't easy. But I learned that if I ran away, I would never discover my purpose.

✦ FROM THE NEST TO DISCIPLESHIP

Over the years, I understood that my mission wasn't just to grow, but to help others grow. That's why we've dedicated our lives to teaching, discipling, and guiding those who have also left their shells. Our calling isn't just to fly, but to raise up eagles that inspire others.

The unpredictable nature of God is that we often think our flight will begin immediately, but first He places us in a nest.

There He silently prepares us, disciplines us, corrects us, and strengthens us. Remaining in that place of formation, even if it's uncomfortable, is what guarantees that our flight will not be fleeting, but firm and lasting.

The nest isn't your final destination, it's your training ground. The unpredictable thing is that when you think you've stopped, you're actually being prepared for a flight that will astound the world.

● REFLECTION

The eagle's nest is not a place of eternal comfort, but a training ground. There, young eagles learn to be fed, to spread their wings, and to take flight under the watchful eyes of their parents. In the same way, your church, your journey, and your experiences have been your nest: the place where God has worked in you, shaping your character and strengthening your faith.

You may not have always understood God's ways, but today you recognize that every tear, every wait, and every instruction has been part of the training for flight. Staying in the nest, even when you wanted to escape, has given you firm roots and wings ready to soar.

✎ PRACTICAL EXERCISES FOR THE READER

1. Remember your nest

Make a list of three experiences in your life or ministry that shaped you, even though at the time you didn't understand the purpose.

2. Identify your mentors

Write down the names of people God used as "eagle parents" in your journey. Pray for them and thank them for their impact on your life.

3. Choose to stay

Reflect: In what areas of your life have you wanted to abandon the process? Make a commitment to faithfulness to God and your calling, deciding to remain steadfast until you see fruit.

4. Prepare your own nest

Think of someone you could disciple, teach, or encourage today. Write down one specific action you can take this week that represents "being a nest" for others.

✎ FINAL STATEMENT:

"Lord, thank you for my nest. Although I didn't

always understand it, I know that you formed me there. I choose to remain faithful, to grow, and to be a place of formation for others. I am ready to spread my wings."

CHAPTER 8

📖 THE EAGLE'S RENEWAL: DYING TO FLY AGAIN

The eagle renews itself by plucking out its old feathers, breaking its beak, and letting a new one grow. Likewise, we must die to the old so that the new may take place in our lives.

To die is to leave behind people, customs, thoughts, and habits that do not build us up. It is to unlearn what is bad in order to learn what is above. It is to surrender what we believe sustains us, in order to discover that only God is our true support.

Each stage of my life has asked me to die a little more. And in each death, God has given me a new life.

✦ THE DYING THAT GIVES LIFE

As the eagle ages, it undergoes a difficult but necessary process: it takes refuge in the rock, breaks its beak, plucks out its old feathers, and waits for everything to be renewed. It is a time of pain, but also of new life.

In the Christian life, we also need to die in order to be renewed.

To die is:

- Knowing when to let go of things that no longer build you up.
- Stay away from people and environments that hinder God's purpose.
- To abandon habits and sins that bind.
- learn what is bad and learn what is from above.

Each stage of my life has required me to die a little more: to my desires, to my character, to what I thought I knew. But in each death I have discovered a new level of life in Christ.

✦ THE PRICE OF UNLEARNING

True growth lies not only in learning new things, but also in unlearning old ones. Your mind cannot soar on new wings if it continues to carry out outdated thinking.

We must unlearn:

- The victim mentality.
- The fear of failure.
- The habit of living in comfort.

Only then can we embrace the unpredictability of God: a renewal that no one expected, a flight higher than ever before.

🦅 REFLECTION

To live longer and fly stronger, the eagle must undergo a painful process of renewal: plucking out its old feathers, breaking its beak, and waiting for everything to grow back. It is a lonely and difficult time, but necessary to extend its lifespan and strength.

Similarly, the Christian life requires us to learn to die to the old: habits, thoughts, wounds, and dependencies that no longer allow us to move forward. This process is not comfortable, but it is the path to renewal and true freedom.

Dying does not mean losing, it means letting go of what hinders us from embracing God's newness.

The unpredictability of *Unpredictable: From Hen to Eagle*
While the world believes that death is an end, God makes it the beginning of a stronger, higher, and more glorious flight.

✎ PRACTICAL EXERCISES FOR THE READER

1. Identify the old

Write down three attitudes, habits, or thoughts that you know you must leave behind so that God can renew you.

2. Make an act of surrender

Pray and surrender each of those areas to God, writing a statement of faith next to it: *"Lord, this dies today so that I may live renewed in You."*

3. Create a renovation plan

Write down practical actions that will replace what you left behind (example: replace complaining with gratitude, doubt with prayer).

4. Seek company in the process

Think of someone you trust who can walk with you and help you stay strong in this spiritual renewal.

FINAL STATEMENT:

> *"I choose to die to the old and be renewed in the power of God. Like the eagle, I renew my strength and am ready to fly higher."*

CHAPTER 9

📖 EAGLES THAT INSPIRE OTHERS

A hen lives for herself; an eagle inspires others to fly.

My transformation wasn't just for me. When God broke me out of my shell and taught me to spread my wings, my family decided to fly with me too. I went from being a disciple to a discipler. What began as a personal process ended up being a family and ministry mission.

True triumph lies not in flying alone, but in guiding others to discover their wings. That is the essence of *Unpredictable: From Hen to Eagle* What God does with you never stays with you, but multiplies in those around you.

✦ MY FAMILY ALSO FLEW

Over the years, I realized that my transformation wasn't just for me. As I grew in my faith and discovered my wings, my family began to move forward with me. They, too, decided to walk and fly. What God did in me became an inspiration for them.

The eagle doesn't fly alone: it builds nests high above, protects its young, and then encourages them to spread their own wings. Our calling is similar: to lift up those around us so they may discover their identity in Christ.

✦ FROM DISCIPLE TO DISCIPLER

At first, I was nurtured in the nest of my church, under the discipleship and vision of my pastors. I learned to obey, to persevere, and to serve. But the time came when the same God who raised me up called me to teach, disciple, and guide others.

I went from needing direction to providing it. From breaking out of my shell to helping others do the same. Today, I dedicate my life to nurturing new eagles, because I know my journey wasn't in vain: it was preparation for being an instrument in the lives of others.

✦ SHIPPING: OUR BIGGEST CHALLENGE

I clearly remember the day our pastor proposed that we start a ministry and send us to begin in a new place. We were afraid. It was unfamiliar territory, without resources, starting from scratch. But there I discovered what distinguishes a chicken from an eagle:

- The hen flees from the unknown.
- The eagle says yes, even though it trembles, and asks God to show it the way.

That obedience taught us that there are no limits when God is guiding our flight. It was the most unpredictable step in our lives, but also the most transformative.

✦ THE LEGACY OF AN EAGLE

Living like an eagle isn't just about reaching personal heights, but about inspiring others to do the same. Every disciple made, every family transformed, every church built up, is part of the legacy an eagle leaves behind.

True triumph is not flying alone, but flying alongside others who have also found their wings.

The unpredictability of *Unpredictable: From Hen to Eagle*

Your story never ends with you; it begins with you, but continues with everyone you will help to fly.

✦ REFLECTION

Today I ask you: Who are you inspiring? Does your flight motivate others to spread their wings, or does it keep them trapped in a chicken mentality? Remember: your journey wasn't just for you, but so that others might dare to believe they too can fly.

📌 PRACTICAL EXERCISE FOR THE READER

Make a list of three people God has placed in your life. Ask yourself:

- How can I help them break out of their shell?
- How can I encourage them to spread their wings?
- What testimony of mine can inspire them to fly higher?

Declare aloud:

> *"My flight will be an inspiration to others. I am an eagle that creates new eagles."*

MARÍA ISABEL RODRÍGUEZ

Your unpredictable legacy is not measured only by how high you fly, but by how many dare to fly because they saw your wings spread.

CHAPTER 10

📖 STAY STEADY IN YOUR UNPREDICTABLE FLIGHT

Discovering your wings and daring to fly is a great step, but staying airborne requires even more discipline, vision, and faith in God. Often, the hardest part isn't starting, but persevering when doubts, obstacles, and storms arise.

The eagle's flight is not always comfortable: it must face strong winds, solitary heights, and long distances. But what sustains it is not the ease of the path, but the strength of its wings.

In *Unpredictable: From Hen to Eagle* Staying strong means remembering who you are, why you started, and where God is leading you.

✦ OBSTACLES THAT WILL TRY TO STOP YOUR FLIGHT

- **Fear of failure:** It will make you want to return to the comfort zone.
- **Others' opinions:** will try to clip your wings with criticism and comparisons.
- **Tiredness:** It will whisper to you to give up when you are closest to your goal.
- **Distractions:** They will want to bring your gaze down from heaven and fix it on earthly things.

✦ HOW TO STAY STEADY ON YOUR FLIGHT

1. **Remember your identity:** You're not a chicken, you're an eagle designed for the heights.
2. **Return to the Word:** each time you doubt, feed on God's promises.
3. **Surround yourself with other eagles:** Prolonged loneliness weakens, but companionship strengthens.
4. **Use storms as a springboard:** Don't run away from the strong wind, spread your wings and let yourself be lifted up.
5. **Keep your eyes on the eternal:** Your goal is not earthly, it is heavenly.

✦ REFLECTION

Staying in an unpredictable flight doesn't mean you'll never fall, but rather that each time you fall you'll rise stronger. The hen gives up when she stumbles, the eagle learns, dusts herself off, and tries again until she conquers the sky.

🐦 PRACTICAL EXERCISE FOR THE READER

1. Write down three obstacles that are trying to stop your flight today.
2. Next to each obstacle, write down a Bible promise that will overcome it.
3. Declare aloud each day:

> *"Nothing will stop me, my flight is unpredictable and God holds my wings."*

The hardest part isn't spreading your wings for the first time, but keeping them open when the winds blow against you. But therein lies your greatness: in not giving up, in standing firm, in showing that what began as a chicken can never be reversed, because your destiny is to be an eagle.

Remember: the unpredictable thing is not that you fly, but that you never stop..

CHAPTER 11

📖 EAGLES IN THE BIBLE: LESSONS FROM THE WORD

Scripture shows us that God has always used examples from His creation to teach us principles for life. Among all animals, the eagle holds a special place: a symbol of strength, vision, and victory. The Bible mentions it as a model for the believer who chooses to trust fully in God.

Studying the Word not only strengthens our faith, but also reaffirms our true identity: eagles called to fly high.

◆ 1. RENEW YOUR STRENGTH LIKE THE EAGLE

Isaiah 40:31

> "But those who wait on the Lord will renew their strength; they will soar on wings like eagles;

they will run and not grow weary, they will walk and not be faint."

The prophet Isaiah reminds us that eagles do not depend on their own limited strength, but on the wind currents that lift them up. Likewise, we must rest in God so that His Spirit may propel us forward.

✦ 2. TO BE CARRIED ON EAGLES' WINGS

Exodus 19:4

> *"You yourselves have seen what I did to the Egyptians, and how I carried you on eagles' wings and brought you to myself."*

God tells Israel that He Himself carried them like an eagle carries its young. Studying this passage reminds us that we are not alone: the Lord sustains us in His grace when we feel our strength failing.

✦ 3. THE CARE UNDER THEIR WINGS

Salmo 91:4

> *"He will cover you with his feathers, and under his*

> *wings you will find refuge; his faithfulness will be your shield and rampart."*

The eagle protects its young under its wings. That is how God protects us under His Word. Every time we study the Bible, we are covered with truths that strengthen us and keep us safe from the enemy.

✦ 4. THE EAGLE'S SHARP VISION

Job 39:27–29

> *"Does the eagle soar at your command and make its nest on high? It dwells and resides on the rock, on the summit of the crag and the cliff. From there it stalks its prey; its eyes observe from afar."*

The eagle has exceptional vision. When we study the Word, our spiritual eyes are opened, and we can see beyond the immediate. The Bible gives us eternal perspective and clear direction.

✦ 5. THE CHALLENGE OF FLYING HIGH

Proverbs 30:18-19

> *"Three things are hidden from me; and I do not*
> *know a fourth: the path of an eagle in the air…"*

The flight of the eagle is a mystery. Likewise, the life of the believer who lives by the Word is difficult for the world to understand, because it is not guided by human logic, but by faith.

✦ FINAL REFLECTION

Each biblical passage is a reminder that the Christian life is a call to soar like an eagle: with vision, with renewed strength, with protection under God's wings, and with direction in the midst of the storm.

✐ PRACTICAL EXERCISES

1. Weekly Eagle Study

- Choose one of the verses mentioned (Isaiah 40:31, Exodus 19:4, Psalm 91:4, Job 39:27-29, Proverbs 30:18-19).
- Read it every day for a week, meditate on it, and write down what God speaks to you through that passage.

2. Underline and apply

- Look in your Bible for other passages where birds, wings, or flight are mentioned.
- Write down what each text symbolizes and how you can apply it to your life.

3. Flight Log

- For one week, write in your notebook each night a "moment of flight"—a situation in which you applied the Word to overcome a fear, a negative thought, or a doubt.

4. Share the teaching

- Explain one of these biblical lessons of the eagle to someone close to you (a friend, family member, or brother in faith).
- Talk to that person about how they can also apply it in their life.

FINAL STATEMENT:

> *"The Word of God is my strength and my guide.*
> *Like an eagle, the Bible teaches me to fly higher,*
> *with clear vision and renewed faith."*

CHAPTER 12

📖 UNPREDICTABLE LEADERSHIP: LEADING FROM ABOVE

Being an eagle is not just a privilege, it's a responsibility. When God lifts us up, it's not so we can enjoy the view alone, but so we can learn to guide others from the heights. True leadership comes from example, not from speeches.

The hen may walk surrounded by many, but none inspire her to fly. The eagle, on the other hand, teaches with her life that it is possible to face storms and still soar higher.

Unpredictable leadership is that which surprises because it does not follow the mold of the world: it does not manipulate, it does not control, it does not impose itself... it serves, it loves and it lifts up.

✦ THE SECRET OF UNPREDICTABLE LEADERSHIP

1. **Lead with vision, not with control.** The eagle does not confine its young, it prepares them to fly.
2. **Lead by example, not just with words.** Your wings preach louder than your voice.
3. **To serve in secret.** The best leaders are those who inspire when no one is watching.
4. **Lift others higher than yourself.** Your true success is helping others reach greater heights.

✦ THE RISK OF STAGNATION

A hen can spend her entire life in the coop, content with the bare minimum. Similarly, many leaders stagnate: they love the title, but not the service; they enjoy the position, but not the sacrifice.

Stagnant leadership stifles. Unpredictable leadership inspires.

✦ REFLECTION

God didn't raise you up to be an ordinary leader, but an eagle to guide with heavenly vision. To lead is to take risks, to challenge, to dare to forge a path where others see only impossibilities.

An unpredictable leader is not measured by how many follow him, but by how many discover their own wings thanks to him.

📌 PRACTICAL EXERCISE FOR THE READER

- Make a list of the people who follow you or see you as a role model.
- Ask yourself: Am I being an eagle that inspires, or a hen that stagnates?
- Write down one specific action you will take this week to lift someone higher than you.

Declare aloud:

> *"I wasn't called to lead from the farmyard, but from the heights. My leadership is unpredictable because it comes from the heart of God."*

The unpredictable aspect of your leadership is that, while others expect you to remain grounded, you choose to soar. And there, you don't just fly: you inspire an entire generation to spread their wings and conquer the sky.

CHAPTER 13

📖 LEADING WITH EAGLE WINGS

Leadership isn't measured by titles or positions, but by the ability to inspire, guide, and transform. The difference between living like a chicken and living like an eagle also applies to leadership.

Many leaders stagnate because they get stuck in a chicken mentality: fearful, confined to their comfort zone, content with the familiar. But a true leader is an eagle: they dare to fly high, take risks, and pave the way for others to follow.

Eagle leadership isn't just about holding a position, but about lifting your gaze, embracing God's vision, and having the courage to guide others with firmness and compassion. While chicken leadership gets stuck in the immediate, eagle leadership is able to see beyond and lead others to reach greater heights.

✦ CHICKEN LEADERSHIP: STAGNATION

- Live in the immediate, without a long-range vision.
- It focuses on the corral: on the problems of the moment and on comparing oneself to others.
- He is afraid of the storm and prefers to flee.
- It depends on constant approval to move.
- He falls into a routine and settles for just surviving.

✦ EAGLE LEADERSHIP: VISION AND GROWTH

- Look beyond the present, with a perspective of the future.
- He knows that storms are opportunities to rise.
- He takes the risk with faith, knowing that God has his back.
- It does not depend on human applause, but on God's guidance.
- Invest in training others, raising new eagles.

✦ BIBLICAL EXAMPLE: NEHEMIAH

Nehemiah could have stayed in the comfortable palace as the king's cupbearer (chicken leadership), but he decided to fly high and take on the challenge of rebuilding the walls of Jerusalem (eagle leadership).

- He saw what others did not see.
- He withstood opposition without surrendering.
- He mobilized an entire people towards a common purpose.

✦ EAGLE LEADERSHIP KEYS

1. Clear vision – Proverbs 29:18: "*Where there is no vision, the people perish.*"
2. Courage in the storm – Leading involves facing crises and seeing them as opportunities.
3. Strong character – Eagle leadership does not bend in the face of criticism or rejection.
4. Teaching and discipleship – A true leader does not accumulate followers, he forms new leaders.
5. Persistence – Like the eagle that endures its renewal process, a leader is not afraid to die to the old in order to move forward to the new.

✦ FINAL REFLECTION

Stagnant leadership is like a chicken: limited, fearful, and complacent. Transformational leadership is like an eagle: visionary, courageous, and a multiplier.

📌 PRACTICAL EXERCISE FOR LEADERS:

- Identify in which area of your leadership you are acting like a chicken.
- Make a list of practical actions to start leading like an eagle.
- Pray with your team and declare:

  "We were not called to stagnate in the corral, we were called to fly like eagles and inspire others to do the same."

✦ LESSONS FOR THE READER

1. Don't get stuck in the corral

- Ask yourself: Am I leading from comfort or from vision?
- Identify an area of your life where you have preferred the safe option and dare to take a step of faith.

2. Use the storm to grow

- Think back to a crisis you experienced as a leader.
- Write down three things you learned from that

experience and how you can teach others with that learning.

3. **Invest in training new eagles**

- Make a list of two people God has placed in your life to mentor or inspire you.
- Establish a practical plan to dedicate time to them (prayer, teaching, accompaniment).

4. **Take care of your character.**

- Reflect: How do I react to criticism, rejection, or opposition?
- Ask God to strengthen your character so that you may remain steadfast in the vision without losing love.

5. **Live with eternal vision**

- Write your personal vision of leadership in a short sentence.
- Repeat this vision every morning as a declaration of faith.

Final statement:

"I am a leader with the vision of an eagle. I don't settle for the corral, I fly high and lead others to achieve God's purpose."

CHAPTER 14

📖 THE PRICE OF FLYING HIGH: WHAT NO ONE TELLS YOU ABOUT THE EAGLE'S PATH

Flying high sounds glorious, but few talk about the cost. Most want the heights, but not everyone is willing to pay the price. Being an eagle means facing winds that others can't withstand, leaving behind comforts that others don't want to give up, and going through processes that seem impossible.

The hen never knows that price because she never tries. She stays on the ground, content with crumbs. But the eagle, when she decides to spread her wings, knows that flight has a cost: loneliness, criticism, effort, and faith.

✦ WHAT NOBODY TELLS YOU ABOUT FLYING

1. **There will be loneliness.** Not everyone will

understand your process, and some will stay in the corral while you move forward.
2. **Criticism will come.** Many will point to your wings, but few will recognize the wind that sustains you.
3. **It will demand sacrifice.** To fly high, you will have to give up burdens that not everyone is willing to let go of.
4. **It will require faith.** You won't always see where you're stepping, but you'll know that the sky was designed for you.

✦ THE VALUE OF SACRIFICE

The price of soaring high is not a loss, it's an investment. What you leave behind is nothing compared to what God has in store for you. Every tear shed in obedience becomes height gained in purpose.

Let's remember: the eagle doesn't soar by fleeing the wind, but by using it. What appears to be a burden is, in reality, the force that propels it.

✦ REFLECTION

Soaring high is not for the complacent. It's for those who dare to pay the price of being misunderstood, criticized, and even rejected, but remain steadfast in their calling.

The farmyard offers comfort, but not destiny. Heaven demands sacrifice, but bestows purpose.

📌 PRACTICAL EXERCISE FOR THE READER

1. Write down three things that you find hard to let go of today.
2. Ask yourself: Are they helping me fly or are they keeping me in the pen?
3. Pray and turn it to God: Declare

> *"I'd rather pay the price of heaven than settle for the comfort of the barnyard."*

The price of soaring high is real, but so is the reward. Every sacrifice you make along the way is proof that you were created for more. And when you look back, you'll discover that what you left behind pales in comparison to the greatness of what you achieved.

Because what is truly unpredictable **to go from chicken to eagle** It's not about starting the flight, but about maintaining it, paying the price, and reaching heights that no one thought were possible.

CHAPTER 15

📖 ACHIEVE IT! STEPS TO MAINTAIN THE EAGLE'S FLIGHT

Learning to fly like an eagle is not an automatic destiny, it is an intentional **and unpredictable process** It requires daily decisions, perseverance through the storms, and unwavering faith. Spreading your wings for the first time isn't enough; true victory lies in staying firm at the heights even when the winds turn against you.

This chapter is your unpredictable map: here you will discover how to move forward, what obstacles to overcome, and how to remain stable when doubts try to close the sky.

✦ STEPS TO ACHIEVE IT

1. Recognize your identity in Christ

- You're not a chicken, you were designed to fly.
- Affirm your identity by reading and declaring the Word daily (Ephesians 2:10, 1 Peter 2:9).

2. Break free from the chains of the past

- Forgiveness is the key that opens your wings.
- Write down what still binds you and give it to God in prayer.

3. Focus on the vision

- Eagles don't get distracted in the corral; they fix their gaze on the heights.
- Define your purpose with clear goals aligned with God's will.

4. Surround yourself with other eagles

- The right environment will determine your height.
- Seek mentors, disciples, and friendships that will propel you to new heights.

✦ OBSTACLES YOU MUST OVERCOME

- **The fear of failure**– Remember: failing doesn't make you less, it's part of learning.

- **The criticism of others** Not everyone will understand your flight, but your call does not depend on their approval.
- **Spiritual weariness**– Renew your strength in prayer and in the Word.
- **Comfort**– The familiar may be a safe haven, but it wasn't designed to stop you.

✦ HOW TO STAY PUT WHEN YOU ARRIVE

Reaching high doesn't mean stopping, but to **stand firm in the heights:**

- **Stay humble**– Recognize that your wings always depend on the wind of God.
- **Persevere in prayer**– Height should not distance you from your source, but bring you closer to it.
- **Keep learning**– Every day there is a new level of teaching and purpose in Christ.
- **Multiply**– Don't keep your flight to yourself; inspire and train others to rise like eagles too.

✦ HOW TO RESPOND IN MOMENTS OF DOUBT

We all face uncertainty, but the key is where you focus your attention:

- **Look to Christ, not to the storm** – Mateo 14:30-31.
- **Remember your past victories**– The same God who sustained you before will do so again.
- **Declare the Word**– The Bible is your sword against the thoughts that try to stop your flight.
- **Seek wise counsel**– Don't struggle alone; open your heart to your pastor, mentor, or faith family.

✦ FINAL REFLECTION

The eagle's flight is not just about taking off, but about to **remain unpredictably strong on top. Every** step of faith, every obstacle overcome, and every doubt faced are the fuel God uses to take you higher.

The corral can't hold someone who's already tasted the heights. And the unpredictable thing about this process is that, even if everyone thinks you'll fall, God holds you up to fly even higher.

📌 PRACTICAL EXERCISE FOR YOU:

1. Write down three concrete steps you will take this week to maintain your flight.
2. Identify an obstacle that is still holding you back and face it in prayer.
3. Declare aloud:

"I wasn't created for the farmyard, I was called to the heights. Today I choose to soar like an eagle in Christ! My flight is unpredictable, because God sustains my wings."

CHAPTER 16

📖 WHEN HEAVEN OPENS YOUR WINGS

We all, regardless of beliefs or backgrounds, have something in common: we seek meaning **and purpose.** Perhaps you come from a place of pain, disappointment, empty religiosity, or even atheism. Perhaps you are young and think that life is a colorless routine, that your story has no value, or that no matter what you do, nothing will change.

But let me tell you this with empathy and enthusiasm: **You are not here by chance.** This book came into your hands because heaven wanted to remind you that there is something more for you. No matter who you are or what you believe right now, within you lies a potential for greatness you have yet to discover.

If you read these pages with an open heart, your life will never be the same again.

✦ A MESSAGE FOR THE DISSATISFIED AND SEEKERS

If you're tired of the same old thing, of empty routines and broken promises, this is your moment to open your eyes. It doesn't matter if you come from religion, atheism, or indifference: within you lies a yearning for transcendence. That yearning is not accidental.

The call is not to a religion, it's to a transformation. To be an eagle means to rise from where you were and dare to fly higher, even if you're afraid.

✦ MOTIVATIONAL MESSAGE

The shell of your fears and doubts may seem hard, but it's not eternal. The scars you carry don't limit you; they're marks that you survived. The mistakes you made don't define you; they're part of your learning.

Today, the sky invites you to look beyond what you see:

- You are not a failure, you are a process.
- You are not what others said about you, you are what you were designed to be.

- You are not a chicken locked in a coop, you are an eagle with wings waiting for the right wind.

This is your moment to say: *"Enough is enough, today I spread my wings and dare to fly."*

✦ QUOTES FOR YOUR DAILY LIFE

- *"Your past doesn't determine your flight, your decision today does."*
- *"What seems like a storm today will be a wind that propels you forward tomorrow."*
- *"The pain you feel today is the muscle of your wings forming."*
- *"Even if you're afraid, fly! The sky will hold you up."*
- *"An eagle is never defined by the mud where it fell, but by the sky to which it returns."*
- *"If you read this book with faith and courage, your life will never be the same again."*
- *"What seems like a storm today will be a wind that propels you forward tomorrow."*
- *"The pain you feel today is the muscle of your wings forming."*
- *"You don't have to understand everything to dare to fly."*
- *"God did not create you for the corral of doubt, but for the heaven of freedom."*

- *"Even if you don't believe in yourself, there is still a heaven that believes in you."*

✦ A MESSAGE FOR YOU

To you who are reading this: I don't know what burdens you carry, I don't know if you're disappointed with life, with people, or even with yourself. But I do know one thing: **There is a heaven that believes in you, even if you yourself doubt your worth.**

This book is not just paper and ink; it's a challenge, a key, a push. It's a reminder that you were created for more.

If you decide to live through these pages, if you dare to apply what you find here, your story will have a new chapter: a flight you never thought was possible.

✦ PRACTICAL EXERCISE

1. **Write about your current storm.**– Put a name to what's bothering you.
2. **Transform your storm into wind**– note how that same situation can motivate you.
3. **Choose your life quote**– Take one of the phrases from this chapter and repeat it every morning as your affirmation.

CHAPTER 17

📖 UNPREDICTABLE: THE FLIGHT THAT CHANGES YOUR STORY

Life is unpredictable. None of us imagined all the paths, the pains, the triumphs, and the surprises that have brought us to this moment. But if there's one thing we can be sure of, it's that God always had a plan.

This book isn't just about hatching or learning to fly; it's about recognizing that your story isn't ordinary, that your flight won't be repeated, that your life is unique. To be **unpredictable** It is accepting that although many thought you would never achieve it, heaven has already written another page for you.

✦ CLOSING MESSAGE

Today you receive a call:

- Don't go back to the corral you came from.

- Don't let criticism clip your wings.
- Don't let yourself be limited by what others think of you.
- Live with the certainty that your flight will leave its mark on others.

To be unpredictable is to be a surprise, to be a miracle, to be a sign that God is still raising eagles at this time.

✦ QUOTES FINALES

"Your life is unpredictable when you decide to believe in God."

"A hen lives in the expected, an eagle lives in the impossible."

"Your flight is the signal others were waiting for."

"Heaven doesn't seek perfection, it seeks what is ready."

✦ FINAL EXERCISE

1. Write a letter to your "chicken self", saying goodbye to the fears and chains of the past.
2. Write a letter to your "eagle self", declaring how you will live from now on.
3. Read both letters aloud as a proclamation of your new identity.

✧ FINAL REFLECTION

This book ends, but your flight has only just begun.

You are unpredictable, because no one can stop what God puts inside you.

Spread your wings, because the world has yet to see the best of you.

📌 **Today your flight begins: unpredictable, unstoppable, and unforgettable.**

✧ FINAL REFLECTION

This chapter is your push, your reminder, your sign. It doesn't matter your past, your doubts, or your current situation: **Your wings are ready and the sky is waiting for you.**

> 📌 *If you dare to believe it, if you apply what you read, your life will never be the same again.*

CHAPTER 18

📖 FINAL CHAPTER – YOUR FLIGHT BEGINS TODAY

This book doesn't end here... in fact, it's just beginning. Every page you read was a mirror reflecting back to you that there was always an eagle inside you. Wounds, fear, or insecurity may have made you feel like a chicken trapped in a coop, but God had already designed you to soar.

The eagle's flight is not just a metaphor; it's a way of life. It's about living with vision, weathering storms, trusting in the Word, and being renewed through trials. Now, this final chapter isn't about me, it's about you.

Your story is still being written. This is the time to take everything you've learned and apply it to your life, your family, your ministry, and your leadership. It doesn't matter how many times you've fallen; what matters is that you are called to rise and spread your wings again.

- **Your shell no longer limits you**– Recognize that what once held you back, today becomes a testament to victory.
- **You have a purpose.**– You were not designed to walk in circles, but to fly towards the destiny that God charted.
- **Your flight inspires others**– By experiencing your transformation, you encourage others to come out of their own shells.
- **The process does not end here**– Every day is a new opportunity to learn, grow and spread your wings higher.

YOUR IDENTITY IS NO LONGER THE SAME

- Before you were limited by fear, now you have a vision of victory.
- Before, your wounds held you back; now, they are scars that tell your story.
- You used to think like a chicken, now you live like an eagle.

The transformation has already begun within you, but this is only the beginning of the flight.

WRITE YOUR OWN PROCESS

I want to invite you to take a notebook or some paper and answer honestly:

1. What was my biggest shell and how did I break through it?
2. Which storm lifted me higher instead of destroying me?
3. What wounds can I use today as a testimony to inspire others?
4. Who do I need to guide or encourage so that they too can discover their wings?

Don't ignore these questions. Write them down, answer them, and keep them as a covenant between you and God.

MAKE YOUR STORY A FLIGHT

The world needs your testimony. Others are trapped in shells of fear, and only your voice can show them that freedom exists. Remember: the eagle not only flies, it also teaches others to fly.

So don't be silent, don't hide, don't turn back. Share your journey, preach your message, inspire with your life.

📌 REFLECTION QUESTIONS:

1. What was your shell and how did you break it?
2. What storm lifted you up instead of destroying you?
3. What wounds can you use as testimony today?
4. Who are you inspiring with your flight?

FINAL DECLARATION OF FAITH

I want to invite you to make this declaration with me:

> "Today I choose to leave my chicken mentality behind. I break free from every shell of fear, insecurity, and pain. I declare that I am an eagle in Christ Jesus, that nothing will stop me, that my wings are ready to fly. I will be unstoppable, because I was created for the heights. This is the beginning of my story as an eagle!"

This book isn't just my story, nor the stories of the testimonies you've read. It's also a mirror for you to discover your own. Every wound, every fear, and every fall has been part of your journey. But today you have the opportunity to decide: do you want to stay in your shell or begin to fly like the eagle God created within you?

Remember: This book ends here, but your flight has only just begun.

📖 ADDITIONAL RESOURCES

✦ KEY VERSES FOR YOUR FLIGHT

1. Isaiah 40:31 – *"But those who hope in the Lord will renew their strength. They will soar on wings like eagles; they will run and not grow weary, they will walk and not faint."*
2. 2 Timothy 1:7 – *"For God has not given us a spirit of fear, but of power, and of love, and of self-control."*
3. Romans 8:37 – *"No, in all these things we are more than conquerors through him who loved us."*
4. Philippians 4:13 – *"I can do all things through Christ who strengthens me."*
5. Psalm 91:4 – *"He will cover you with his feathers, and under his wings you will find refuge."*

📖 ADDITIONAL RESOURCES

✦ DECLARATIONS OF FAITH

- I am an eagle in Christ, designed for the heights.
- My past does not define my future; God has already written my purpose.
- Every storm pushes me to fly higher.
- I don't live in fear, I live in faith.
- My wounds are testimonies of victory.
- I will never give up, because I was created to win.

✦ SPACES FOR YOUR REFLECTIONS

📌 My shell that I need to break:

The storms that drive me today:

📌 **People I want to inspire with my flight:**

📌 **My final statement as an eagle:**

ABOUT THE AUTHOR

María Isabel Rodríguez was born in Humacao, Puerto Rico on February 5th, into a humble but hardworking family. The eldest of three sisters and one brother, she learned the value of responsibility, discipline, and perseverance from a young age. Her childhood was marked by adversity, but that same adversity fueled her dreams, expanded her vision, and transformed every place she encountered.

On October 16, 2013, in the city of Philadelphia, she gave her life to Christ at the First Christian Missionary Church, under the pastorate of Reverend José M. Roque. From that moment, her life took a radical turn, going from being a dreamer with a longing for change, to a woman of faith, called and set apart by God to guide others.

María Isabel is a wife and mother of three children, all of whom serve in ministry. Together they form a purpose-driven family, committed to God's calling, working together in service and vision to impact this generation.

She is a tireless innovator, entrepreneur, and community leader, owning several businesses and ministries that inspire others to grow. She possesses extensive academic and ministerial training that she always puts at the service of her community.

✦ PUBLISHED BOOKS

María Isabel Rodríguez is also the author of several inspirational and training books that have impacted lives:

- 📖 *Today I am stronger than yesterday*
- 📖 *Giving up is not an option*
- 📖 *Beyond Yesterday's Strength*
- 📖 *Giving Up is Not an Option*
- 📖 *Let the world hear!*
- 📖 *Let the World Hear*

All these titles are available at **Amazon** Or you can request them directly by sending an email to airamisabel05@gmail.com for more information.

✦ STUDIES AND ACADEMIC PREPARATION

- University of Puerto Rico – Bachelor of Arts in Interdisciplinary Pre-Legal Studies

- University College of Gurabo, P.R. – Associate Degree in Criminal Justice
- Global University – Berea Bible School – Diploma in Ministerial Studies with a Specialization in Leadership (Licensed Minister)
- DeVry University – Bachelor of Business Administration
- Global University – Doctorado en Ministry Leadership

✦ CERTIFICATIONS AND SPECIALIZATIONS

- Coaching in Business Administration (Women Business Center)
- Coach, Speaker and Trainer certified by the John Maxwell Team
- Certified Translator (Oxford University)

✦ LEADERSHIP AND MINISTRY

- Founder and owner of several companies in the U.S. and Puerto Rico.
- Senior Pastor of El Legado Church, a ministry where she empowers lives to grow in faith, character, and purpose.

- Speaker, author, and mentor who inspires others to break out of their shells and fly like eagles.

  Her life is a testament that small beginnings do not determine destiny, and that God can raise up the extraordinary from the simple.

www.ingramcontent.com/pod-product-compliance
Lightning Source LLC
Chambersburg PA
CBHW070258100426
42743CB00011B/2256